50 WAYS WITH

BEEF

50 WAYS WITH

BEEF

KATHARINE BLAKEMORE

LITTLE BROWN
AND COMPANY
BOSTON • TORONTO • LONDON

A Little Brown Book

Little, Brown and Company (UK)
Brettenham House, Lancaster Place, London WC2E 7EN

First Published in 1991
First Published in the UK by Little, Brown and Company in 1997

Lansdowne Publishing Pty Ltd
Sydney, Australia

ISBN 0-316-64418-8

A CIP catalogue record for this book is available from
the British Library

Design: Kathie Baxter Smith
Photography by Andrew Elton
Food Styling by Mary Harris
Set in Goudy on Quark Xpress by Bronwyn Hilton
Printed in Singapore by Tien Wah Press (Pte) Ltd

Front cover photograph: Beef with Orange Teriyaki Marinade, recipe page 34
Page 2: Beef Fajitas with Two Salsas, recipe page 20
Pages 8–9: Samosas with Mint and Yogurt Raita, recipe page 96
Back cover photograph: Cold Foccacia, recipe page 48

CONTENTS

INTRODUCTION

This book is a response to the constant need for fresh, exciting recipes for beef that require minimum effort and time and always taste great. Beef makes the basis of a good satisfying meal. It is high in protein as well as being a very effective source of iron and the B vitamins that are so essential to healthy family living. There is a deliberate emphasis on light and healthy dishes that avoid the "meat and three vegetables" distinction and, with a little imagination and this book, the variety of dishes you can produce is endless. These recipes show how you can enhance beef with many fresh herbs, spices, pastes and marinades, how to combine beef with interesting ingredients in delicious stir-frys, salads, curries, steamboats and also provide wonderful accompaniments — sauces, sambals, raitas, salsas, crusts and stuffings.

Beef is cooked either by dry heat with such methods as broiling (grilling), roasting or stir-frying, or by the moist heat method where meat is pot-roasted or casseroled. As well as the instructions and hints set out in each recipe, these cooking methods are described in detail on page 110 to ensure that you are rewarded with perfect beef every time you choose to cook it.

For cooking purposes, beef is usually defined by the part of the animal it comes from. The forequarter joints from the front are tougher, coarser-grained and therefore cheaper cuts. They usually require the slow moist cooking methods. These cuts include chuck, blade, shin, and brisket. The ribs, which also come from the front end, are suitable for roasting. The hindquarter cuts include rump, sirloin, and topside, these are more tender and are served as steaks or used for the quicker cooking methods.

When buying beef, look for meat that is bright pink to red with no excess blood coming from it. Also, buy beef that is as lean as possible. "Trim" beef cuts are now available where all the fat has been removed. Although it is sometimes necessary to add a little fat when cooking beef it should be in the form of a vegetable oil or low fat polyunsaturated margarine — a much healthier alternative to animal fat.

Always buy the appropriate cut of meat for the recipe you are using. For instance, rump steak will toughen if used in a casserole-type recipe.

Once the beef has been purchased it should be kept as cool as possible. If it is necessary to buy meat for dinner during your lunch hour, make sure the meat is kept cold in a cool bag. Try to cook meat on the day of purchase. If this is not possible remove from the original packaging, put it in a dish, cover with foil and keep in the coldest part of the refrigerator. Meat should not be kept for more than two to three days. If meat is to be kept overnight then consider marinading it. The meat will then absorb the tastes of the marinade and in some cases the marinade will also help to tenderize the beef.

Beef is a very adaptable meat, and as well as being suitable for many cooking methods it combines well with other tastes from light and fruity to the intense and spicy oriental. These recipes draw on a wealth of cooking tradition from beef-eating nations around the world: try Balti Beef, Beef Rendang with Cucumber Raita and Banana Sambal, Cajun Blackened Steaks, Singapore Noodles, Stuffed Vine Leaves, Sukiyaki or Thai Beef Salad. Of course, there are still old favorites like Beef and Mushroom Phyllo Pies, lasagne, burgers, Quick and Easy Steak Sauces, pot roasts, Beef Stroganoff or Boeuf Bourguignonne.

Be it for entertaining or family dining, you will never tire of beef so long as this book is handy. Enjoy.

THE RECIPES

BALTI BEEF

2 tablespoons ghee or vegetable
    oil
1 onion, chopped
1 teaspoon grated fresh ginger
1 teaspoon paprika
1 teaspoon turmeric
1 teaspoon garlic puree
1 tablespoon mild curry paste
1 cup (8 fl oz, 250 ml) beef stock
salt and freshly ground black
    pepper
1$^{1}/_{2}$ lb (700 g) rib-eye steak, cut
    into small thin slices
8 oz (225 g) small okra, ends
    removed
15 oz (425 g) can garbanzos
    (chickpeas), drained
9 oz (250 g) fresh young English
    spinach
2 teaspoons garam marsala
2 teaspoons dried fenugreek
    leaves, if available
4 naan breads to serve

Heat 1 tablespoon ghee in a small pan, add onion and ginger and cook for 2–3 minutes until onion is soft. Add paprika and turmeric, cook for 1 minute, then stir in garlic puree, curry paste, stock, salt and pepper. Bring to a boil then simmer uncovered for about 10 minutes until liquid has been reduced to half.

Heat remaining ghee in a large frying pan or wok, stir-fry the beef and okra for about 2 minutes to seal the meat, then add garbanzos, spinach and curry sauce and mix well. Cook gently until spinach has wilted and garbanzos have heated through, then stir in garam marsala and fenugreek leaves.

Divide between 4 warmed Indian individual serving dishes or other individual dishes and eat with the naan bread.

Preparation time 15 minutes

Cooking time 15 minutes

Serves 4

BEEF AND BEAN SALAD

9 oz (250 g) green (French) beans,
  ends removed
1 oz (30 g) fresh white crustless
  bread
4 oz (115 g) walnuts
1¹/₂ cups (12 fl oz, 350 ml) beef
  stock
salt and freshly ground black
  pepper
12–16 slices cold roast beef
8 oz (225 g) can red kidney beans
2 tablespoons walnut oil
2 teaspoons paprika

Cook green beans in lightly salted boiling water for 3 minutes. Drain then cool under cold running water. Drain well.

Put bread, walnuts, stock, salt and pepper into a blender or food processor and blend until smooth.

Arrange beef around the edge of a large round serving plate. Pile green beans into the middle of the plate, then arrange kidney beans between the beef and green beans. Drizzle walnut sauce over the salad.

Heat walnut oil and paprika to allow the tastes to blend (a microwave is ideal for this), then sprinkle over the blended sauce.

Preparation time 15 minutes

Cooking time 5 minutes

Serves 4

BEEF AND MUSHROOM PHYLLO PIES

1 onion, chopped
8 oz (225 g) field mushrooms,
  chopped
salt and freshly ground black
  pepper
2 cloves garlic, crushed
1 tablespoon sunflower oil
8 slices skirt steak, about 3–4 oz
  (85–115 g) each, beaten flat
4 teaspoons creamed horseradish
1¼ cups (10 fl oz, 300 ml) beef
  stock
1 tablespoon mushroom ketchup
  (sauce) or Worcestershire sauce
1 tablespoon cornstarch
  (cornflour)
4 sheets phyllo pastry
2 oz (60 g) low-fat
  polyunsaturated margarine,
  melted

Cook onion, mushrooms and garlic in oil in a frying pan until soft. Remove from pan with slotted spoon, leaving any excess juices in pan. Season mushrooms with salt and pepper.

Spread each slice of skirt steak with ½ teaspoon creamed horseradish, divide the mushroom mixture between the steaks and roll up. Put two steak rolls into each of 4 small ovenproof dishes with the joins underneath.

Mix stock, mushroom ketchup and cornstarch together, pour into the pan with excess juices, mix well, then bring to a boil. Divide the sauce between the 4 dishes and cover with foil.

Preheat oven to 350°F (180°C, Gas Mark 4). Cook rolls in oven for about 40 minutes. Remove dishes from oven and increase oven heat to 400°F (200°C, Gas Mark 6).

Brush phyllo pastry with margarine, then cut pastry into strips about 1½ inches (4 cm) wide. Drop pastry strips randomly over beef rolls, making sure the whole of each dish is covered. Return to the oven for a further 10–15 minutes until pastry is crisp and browned.

Preparation time 15 minutes

Cooking time 1 hour

Serves 4

Beef and Potato Mille-feuille

2 oz (60 g) low-fat
    polyunsaturated margarine
1 small onion, finely chopped
1 small head Florence fennel 4 oz
    (115 g), finely chopped
1 small dessert apple, about 4 oz
    (115 g), peeled, cored and
    finely chopped
2 oz (60 g) fresh white
    breadcrumbs
1 tablespoon chopped fresh dill
1 tablespoon chopped fresh
    parsley
2 oz (60 g) salted cashew nuts,
    finely chopped
salt and ground black pepper
1 egg yolk
1 lb 6 oz (625 g) long, narrow
    piece roasting beef
1 tablespoon all-purpose (plain)
    flour
1 cup (8 fl oz, 250 ml) beef stock
sprigs of fresh dill to garnish

Potato pancakes:
1 onion, finely chopped
2–3 tablespoons sunflower oil
1 1/2 lb (700 g) floury potatoes,
    peeled

Melt half the margarine in a pan and cook onion, fennel and apple for 2–3 minutes until soft. Stir in breadcrumbs, dill, parsley, nuts, salt, pepper and egg yolk and stand to cool.

Preheat oven to 400°F (200°C, Gas Mark 6). Cut a deep pocket in beef. Shape fennel stuffing into a sausage, stuff into beef and secure with string. Spread meat with remaining margarine, place in a baking dish and cook in oven for about 1 hour.

Meanwhile, make potato pancakes. Cook onion in 1 tablespoon oil until soft. Grate potatoes, squeeze out excess moisture with paper towels. Add to onion with salt and pepper and mix well.

Heat oil in large frying pan. Drop 4 large tablespoons of potato into pan flattening each into a neat round of about 4 inches (10 cm) in diameter. Cook for about 2 minutes each side until brown then make eight more in the same way. Keep warm.

Remove meat from baking dish and keep warm. Put dish onto stove, stir flour into meat juices and cook for 1 minute. Add stock and bring to a boil.

Remove string from meat, cut into 8 slices. Layer 2 slices of meat between 3 potato pancakes to form 4 stacks.

Strain sauce and divide between 4 warmed plates. Put a mille-feuille on each plate and garnish with sprigs of dill.

Preparation time 30 minutes

Cooking time 1 hour 10 minutes

Serves 4

BEEF AND TROPICAL FRUIT KEBABS

15 oz (425 g) can pineapple
   chunks
4 tablespoons mango chutney
2 tablespoons balsamic vinegar
2 tablespoons sunflower oil
1 teaspoon ground ginger
salt and freshly ground black
   pepper
1¹/₄ lb (550 g) rump or sirloin
   steak, cut into large cubes
1 large mango, peeled and cut
   into cubes
2 kiwi fruit, peeled and cut into
   cubes
2 large firm bananas, peeled and
   thickly sliced
1 teaspoon cornstarch (cornflour)

Drain juice from pineapple into a large ceramic or glass bowl. Add chutney, vinegar, oil, ginger, salt and pepper. Mix well and add steak. Cover and chill for 4 hours or overnight.

Preheat broiler (grill) or barbecue to high. Thread the steak cubes onto 4 large kebab skewers alternating with pieces of fruit. Brush with marinade then cook for about 5 minutes, turning once and brushing with marinade.

Put remaining marinade into a small pan. Add cornstarch, mix well, and bring to a boil. Simmer for 1 minute and serve with kebabs.

Preparation time 10 minutes plus marinating time

Cooking time 5 minutes

Serves 4

BEEF FAJITAS WITH TWO SALSAS

1 clove garlic, sliced
1 large onion, sliced
1 large red bell pepper (capsicum),
    seeded and sliced
1 large green bell pepper
    (capsicum), seeded and sliced
1 jalapeño pepper, chopped, or
    1 teaspoon hot chili sauce
2 tablespoons olive oil
1¹/₂ lb (700 g) rib-eye or rump
    steak, cut into thin strips
juice of 1 lime
salt and freshly ground black
    pepper
flour tortillas, sour cream and
    shredded lettuce to serve

Three tomato salsa:
1 teaspoon crushed coriander seeds
1 small red (salad) onion, chopped
2 medium red tomatoes, diced
2 medium yellow tomatoes, diced
4 oz (115 g) sun-dried tomatoes in
    oil, drained and chopped
1 tablespoon oil from sun-dried
    tomato jar
1–2 teaspoons jalapeño pepper sauce
1 tablespoon chopped cilantro
    (fresh coriander leaves)

Avocado salsa:
1 ripe avocado
2 tablespoons low-fat sour cream
1 clove garlic, crushed
1 tablespoon lime juice
2–3 drops Tabasco sauce
grated rind of 1 lime

In a large frying pan or wok stir-fry garlic, onion, bell peppers and jalapeño pepper in oil for 2–3 minutes until soft. Add beef and cook for a further 2–3 minutes until beef is cooked through. Stir in lime juice, salt and pepper.

Three tomato salsa: Combine all ingredients in a bowl, mix well and transfer to a small serving dish.

Avocado salsa: Mash avocado with sour cream. Stir in garlic, lime juice, Tabasco sauce, salt and pepper. Transfer to a small serving dish and sprinkle lime rind over the top.

Transfer beef to a warm serving dish and serve with flour tortillas, salsas, sour cream and shredded lettuce.

Preparation time 25 minutes

Cooking time 10 minutes

Serves 4

BEEF PLATTER WITH THREE DIPPING SAUCES

1 lb (450 g) lean ground (minced)
    beef
1 small onion, grated
1 egg, beaten
3 tablespoons low-fat (skim) milk
1 tablespoon all-purpose (plain)
    flour
salt and ground black pepper
1 frilly-leaved lettuce (lollo rosso
    or curly endive)
12 oz (350 g) thinly sliced cold
    roast beef
12 oz (350 g) thinly sliced smoked
    beef or pastrami
1 red bell pepper (capsicum),
    seeded and cut into strips
1/2 cucumber, cut into strips
1 large carrot, peeled and cut into
    strips
1 bunch radishes
1 baby cauliflower, cut into florets
1 Belgian endive (witloof), core
    removed and leaves separated

Mango and walnut dipping sauce:
4 tablespoons mango chutney
juice of 1/2 lemon
2 tablespoons walnut oil
1 tablespoon chopped walnuts

Sun-dried tomato and caper
    dipping sauce:
2/3 cup (5 fl oz, 150 ml) low-fat
    plain (natural) yogurt
2 oz (50 g) sun-dried tomatoes
    in oil, cut into strips
1 tablespoon oil from sun-dried
    tomato jar
1 tablespoon capers
salt and freshly ground black
    pepper

Blue cheese and celery dipping
    sauce:
4 oz (115 g) creamy blue cheese
    (dolcelatte or pipo creme)
3 tablespoons low-fat crème
    fraîche
2 tablespoons low-fat
    mayonnaise
1 stick celery, finely chopped
freshly ground black pepper

Preparation time 30 minutes

Cooking time 20 minutes

Serves 6–8

Preheat oven to 400°F (200°C, Gas Mark 6). Combine first 6 ingredients in a large bowl. Shape into small balls. Put onto a non-stick baking sheet, cook in oven for 20 minutes. Stand until cold.

Line a large platter with lettuce leaves. Decoratively arrange roast beef, smoked beef, meat balls, raw vegetables and dishes of dipping sauce on the lettuce.

Mango and walnut dip: Combine chutney, juice, walnut oil, salt and pepper in a small serving bowl. Sprinkle with chopped walnuts.

Sun-dried tomato and caper dip: Combine all ingredients in a small serving bowl.

Blue cheese and celery dip: Mash blue cheese, crème fraîche and mayonnaise in a small serving bowl. Stir in celery and pepper.

RENDANG WITH CUCUMBER RAITA AND BANANA SAMBAL

2 oz (60 g) tamarind, soaked for
    10 minutes in 6 tablespoons
    boiling water
1 red chili pepper, seeded and
    chopped
1 teaspoon chili powder
2 onions, chopped
2 cloves garlic
2 in (5 cm) piece root ginger, peeled
1 teaspoon ground turmeric
1 tablespoon coriander seeds
1 teaspoon cumin seeds
1 stalk lemon grass
1 1/2 cups (12 fl oz, 350 ml)
    coconut cream
salt and ground black pepper
1 tablespoon sunflower oil
1 3/4 lb (800 g) lean braising steak
    (chuck or blade), diced
1 tablespoon curry leaves to
    garnish
Basmati rice and poppadums to
    serve

Cucumber raita:
1/2 cucumber, cut into small dice
2/3 cup (5 fl oz, 150 ml) low-fat
    plain (natural) yogurt
4 scallions (shallots), chopped

Banana sambal:
2/3 cup (5 fl oz, 150 ml) coconut
    cream
1 large green banana, thinly
    sliced
salt and freshly ground black
    pepper
1 tablespoon unsweetened
    (desiccated) coconut, toasted

Strain tamarind, discarding solids. Put tamarind water into a blender or food processor with remaining ingredients except oil and beef and blend to combine.

Heat oil in a large frying pan. Cook beef for 2–3 minutes until very brown. Add blended sauce to pan. Mix well. Bring to a boil and simmer gently, uncovered, for about 40 minutes, stirring occasionally. Only a little liquid should remain.

Cook a further 10 minutes, stirring to prevent sticking, until all liquid has evaporated and the meat is just coated with spicy sauce. Transfer to a serving dish, sprinkle with curry leaves and serve with rice, poppadums, cucumber raita and sambal.

Cucumber raita: Mix cucumber with yogurt, salt and pepper. Put into a small serving dish and sprinkle with onions.

Banana sambal: Put coconut cream, banana, salt and pepper into a small pan. Heat gently and transfer to a small, warmed serving dish and sprinkle with toasted coconut.

Preparation time 25 minutes

Cooking time 55 minutes

Serves 4

Beef Salad Niçoise

1 large eggplant (aubergine), ends removed and cut into thick strips
4 zucchini (courgettes), ends removed and cut into thick strips
1 large red bell pepper (capsicum), seeded and cut into thick strips
1 large green bell pepper (capsicum), seeded and cut into thick strips
3 tablespoons olive oil
4 tomatoes, quartered
1 bunch scallions (shallots), trimmed
4–5 tablespoons black olive paste
12–16 slices rare roast beef
salt and freshly ground black pepper
1 tablespoon garlic vinegar

Preheat broiler (grill) to high. Toss eggplant, zucchini and bell peppers in 2 tablespoons oil. Put into a baking pan that fits under broiler and broil (grill) for 8–10 minutes, stirring occasionally, until vegetables are soft and lightly browned. Transfer to paper towels and let stand until cold.

Brush tomatoes and onions with remaining oil. Broil for about 3 minutes, turning once. Transfer to paper towels, let stand until cold.

Spread olive paste on one end of each slice of beef. Arrange beef in the middle of a serving platter with the olive paste alternately to the left and right. Put half the eggplant mixture down each side of the beef. Arrange tomatoes and onions on top of the other vegetables. Season with salt and pepper and sprinkle with garlic vinegar.

Preparation time 15 minutes

Cooking time 15 minutes

Serves 4

BEEF STROGANOFF

1¹/₄ lb (550 g) lean steak (fillet or
    rump), cut into thin strips
1 tablespoon all purpose (plain)
    flour
1 tablespoon paprika
1 tablespoon sunflower oil
¹/₂ oz (15 g) low-fat
    polyunsaturated margarine
1 large onion, sliced
12 oz (350 g) button mushrooms
    (champignons)
1 tablespoon dry sherry
1 tablespoon Worcestershire sauce
salt and freshly ground black
    pepper
¹/₂ cup (4 fl oz/120 ml) low-fat
    sour cream
noodles tossed with poppy seeds to
    serve

Coat steak strips in a combination of flour and paprika.
Heat oil in a large frying pan or wok, quickly fry beef for
1–2 minutes, stirring constantly until browned. Remove
from pan.

Melt margarine in pan, add onion and mushrooms and cook
for about 5 minutes until onion is soft. Return steak to pan
and add sherry, Worcestershire sauce, salt and pepper. Stir well
and bring to a boil. Remove from heat and lightly stir in sour
cream to make a marbled effect. Serve immediately with
noodles tossed with poppy seeds.

Preparation time 10 minutes

Cooking time 10 minutes

Serves 4

BEEF TAGINE WITH COUSCOUS

1 teaspoon ground ginger
1 teaspoon ground cinnamon
1/2 teaspoon ground allspice
pinch ground cloves
1 1/2 lb (700 g) lean braising steak
    (chuck or blade), cut into chunks
1 onion, sliced
1 clove garlic, crushed
1 tablespoon olive oil
grated rind and juice 1 lemon
2 tablespoons quince jelly or honey
1 cup (8 fl oz, 250 ml) prune juice
1 teaspoon harissa or sambal oelek
    or cayenne to taste
salt and freshly ground pepper

Couscous:
8 oz (225 g) couscous
2 1/2 cups (20 fl oz, 600 ml) water
2 tablespoons olive oil
1 onion, chopped
1 teaspoon ground cinnamon
1/2 teaspoon ground allspice
1 teaspoon ground turmeric
1 tablespoon ground cumin
1 teaspoon ground coriander
1 teaspoon dried mint
2/3 cup (3 oz, 85 g) pistachio nuts
2/3 cup (3 oz, 85 g) pine nuts
sprigs cilantro (fresh coriander
    leaves) to garnish

Mix together ginger, cinnamon, allspice and cloves and rub into beef.

Preheat oven to 325°F (170°C, Gas Mark 3). Cook onion and garlic in oil in a heavy-based casserole dish until soft, add beef and cook for 2–3 minutes until beef is browned. Add lemon rind and juice, quince jelly, prune juice, harissa and salt, and bring to a boil. Transfer to oven and cook for 1–1 1/4 hours until meat is tender.

When meat has been in the oven for about 1/2 hour, prepare couscous.

Boil 2 1/2 cups water, pour into a large bowl with couscous and let it stand for about 10 minutes until all water is absorbed.

Heat oil in a frying pan and fry onion until soft. Add remaining ingredients, stir well and cook for 2–3 minutes. Add onion to couscous and mix well. Transfer couscous to a lightly greased ring tin or spread over a serving plate. Cover with foil and put into the bottom of oven until meat is cooked.

Remove couscous from oven, turn out of ring tin (if using) onto a serving plate. Spoon beef into the middle of the couscous and garnish with cilantro.

Preparation time 20 minutes

Cooking time 1–1 1/4 hours

Serves 4

BEEF VINDALOO

1 teaspoon turmeric
2 teaspoons black mustard seeds
2 teaspoons grated fresh ginger
2 cloves garlic, crushed
1 tablespoon vindaloo curry paste
3 tablespoons white wine vinegar
2 teaspoons ground coriander
2 teaspoons ground cumin
2 onions, chopped
1¹/₂ lb (700 g) lean braising steak
   (chuck or blade)
2 tablespoons ghee or sunflower
   oil
1 14 oz (400 g) can peeled
   tomatoes
1 lb (450 g) potatoes, diced
1 cup (8 fl oz, 250 ml) beef stock
salt and freshly ground black
   pepper
Basmati rice and chapatis to serve

Mix together turmeric, mustard seeds, ginger, garlic, curry paste, vinegar, coriander and cumin to make a thick paste.

In a large saucepan with a cover, fry onion and beef in ghee until beef is brown. Stir in paste and cook for 2–3 minutes, stirring constantly. Add tomatoes and juice from can, potatoes, stock, salt and pepper. Bring to a boil, reduce heat, cover pan and simmer gently for about 1 hour, stirring occasionally, until meat is tender.

Transfer to a warmed serving dish and serve with Basmati rice and chapatis.

Preparation time 20 minutes

Cooking time 1 hour

Serves 4

BEEF WITH ORANGE TERIYAKI MARINADE

grated rind and juice of 1 orange
1 small onion, finely chopped
1 clove garlic, crushed
1 tablespoon grated fresh ginger
3 tablespoons soy sauce
2 teaspoons crushed coriander
  seeds
2 teaspoons crushed cumin seeds
salt and freshly ground black
  pepper
1¹/₂ lb (700 g) piece beef flank
8 oz (225 g) dried fruit salad
  (pears, prunes, apricots)
1 cinnamon stick
6 cloves
1 teaspoon crushed juniper berries
1 cup (8 fl oz, 250 ml) red wine
1 oz (30 g) soft brown sugar
1 cup (8 fl oz, 250 ml) water

Mix together orange rind, juice, onion, garlic, ginger, soy sauce, coriander, cumin, salt and pepper. Coat beef on both sides with this mixture. Place in a shallow ceramic or glass dish, cover and chill for at least 4 hours or overnight. Put dried fruit into a small pan with cinnamon stick, cloves, juniper berries, wine, sugar and water. Bring to a boil, simmer for 3 minutes and let stand for 4 hours or overnight.

Preheat broiler (grill) to high.

Remove meat from marinade, reserving marinade, and put onto a rack over a pan. Broil (grill) for about 5–6 minutes each side (flank is best served slightly rare).

Remove and discard cinnamon stick, cloves and juniper berries from dried fruit. Add reserved marinade to the fruit, bring to a boil. Simmer for 2–3 minutes.

Cut beef into thick slices, diagonally, put onto a warmed serving platter and arrange fruit around the beef.

Preparation time 15 minutes plus marinating time

Cooking time 15 minutes

Serves 4

BOEUF BOURGUIGNONNE

1¹/₂ lb (700 g) lean braising steak, (chuck or blade)
2 tablespoons olive oil
1 cup (8 fl oz, 250 ml) red wine
1 cup (8 fl oz, 250 ml) beef stock
2 sprigs fresh thyme
salt and freshly ground black pepper
8 oz (225 g) spring onions (shallots)
1 head garlic, divided into cloves
6 oz (175 g) wild mushrooms (chanterelle, morel, or girolle) or button mushrooms (champignons)
sprigs fresh thyme to garnish

Cut meat into 16 large chunks and brown in 1 tablespoon oil in a covered pan. Add wine, bring to a boil and simmer, uncovered, until sauce is reduced by half. Add stock, thyme, salt and pepper. Cover pan and simmer gently for about 40 minutes until meat is tender.

Boil unpeeled onions and garlic cloves in lightly salted water for about 3 minutes, drain, cool and peel.

Preheat oven to 425°F (220°C, Gas Mark 7). Brush onions and garlic with remaining oil. Put onto a baking sheet and roast for about 10 minutes.

When meat is cooked, remove from stock and keep warm. Boil stock until reduced to 1 cup (8 fl oz, 250 ml). Discard thyme, add mushrooms and cook for 2 minutes more.

Place 4 pieces of beef in the middle of each of four warmed plates. Pour sauce and mushrooms around meat and garnish with onions, garlic cloves and fresh thyme.

Preparation time 15 minutes

Cooking time 50 minutes

Serves 4

BORSCH

1 red (salad) onion, chopped
1 lb (450 g) lean braising steak
  (chuck, blade), cut into small
  cubes
1 lb (450 g) raw beets (beetroot),
  peeled and grated
12 oz (350 g) red cabbage, finely
  shredded
5 cups (40 fl oz, 1.2 l) beef stock
2 tablespoons red wine vinegar
1 tablespoon ketchup (tomato
  sauce)
salt and freshly ground black
  pepper
1 teaspoon dried thyme
8 oz (225 g) firm waxy potatoes,
  peeled and diced
1/2 cup (4 fl oz, 125 ml) low-fat
  sour cream
1 teaspoon fennel seeds
2 teaspoons chopped fresh dill

Cook onion and beef in oil in a large covered pan until beef is brown. Add beets, cabbage, stock, vinegar, ketchup, salt, pepper and thyme. Bring to a boil, reduce heat and simmer for 40 minutes.

Add potatoes to pan and cook for further 10 minutes.

Divide the soup between 6 warmed soup bowls. Put 1 tablespoon sour cream into the middle of each, then sprinkle with fennel seeds and dill.

Preparation time 15 minutes

Cooking time 55 minutes

Serves 4–6

CAJUN BLACKENED STEAKS

2 teaspoons paprika
1 teaspoon ground black pepper
1/2 teaspoon cayenne pepper
2 teaspoons garlic salt
2 teaspoons dried thyme
2 teaspoons dried oregano
1 teaspoon sugar
4 sirloin or porterhouse steaks,
    about 6–8 oz (170–225 g) each
2 tablespoons melted butter
4 teaspoons chopped chives to
    garnish
Dirty rice timbales:
1 onion, chopped
4 sticks celery, chopped
1 red bell pepper (capsicum),
    seeded and chopped
1 clove garlic, crushed
1 tablespoon sunflower oil
1 teaspoon ground cumin
6 oz (175 g) easy cook long-grain
    rice
2 1/2 cups (20 fl oz, 600 ml) beef
    stock
salt and freshly ground black
    pepper
8 oz (225 g) chicken livers, finely
    chopped

Mix together paprika, black pepper, cayenne, garlic salt, thyme, oregano and sugar. Reserve 4 teaspoons of spice mixture for cooking rice.

Dip steaks into melted butter and coat each side with spice mixture. Cover and let stand while rice is cooking.

For dirty rice timbales: Cook onion, celery, pepper and garlic in oil in a large pan with a cover until soft. Add reserved spices, cumin and rice and stir well until rice is coated with spices. Add stock, salt and pepper and bring to a boil. Reduce heat, cover pan and cook for about 20 minutes until all liquid is absorbed. Remove pan from heat and add chicken livers. Mix well, re-cover pan and let stand for 5 minutes.

Preheat oven to 350°F (180°C, Gas Mark 4). Divide rice between eight lightly greased ramekin dishes, cover with foil and put into oven while cooking steaks.

Heat a large heavy-based frying pan until very hot. Cook steaks for 2–3 minutes each side depending on how you like your steaks.

Transfer steaks to four warmed plates. Turn out a ramekin of rice at each side of steak and serve sprinkled with chopped chives.

Preparation time 20 minutes

Cooking time 30 minutes

Serves 4

CARIBBEAN BEEF STEW

1 onion, sliced
2 cloves garlic, crushed
8 oz (225 g) can tomatoes,
    chopped and juice reserved
1 teaspoon dried thyme
1 teaspoon ground allspice
1 teaspoon celery salt
1¹/₂ lb (700 g) braising steak
    (chuck or top rump) diced
2 tablespoons sunflower oil
1 teaspoon soft brown sugar
1 cup (8 fl oz, 250 ml) beef stock
2 tablespoons rum
2 tablespoons Tabasco sauce
1 small red bell pepper (capsicum),
    seeded and sliced
1 tablespoon cornstarch
    (cornflour)
freshly ground black pepper
celery leaves to garnish
rice mixed with peas to serve

In a large ceramic or glass bowl mix together the onion, garlic, tomatoes and juice from can, thyme, allspice and celery salt. Add beef, mix well, cover and chill for 4 hours or overnight.

Strain beef and reserve marinade. Heat oil in a large covered pan, add sugar and beef and cook until beef is brown. Add stock, rum, Tabasco and reserved marinade to pan. Bring to boil, cover pan, reduce heat and simmer gently for 40 minutes.

Add bell pepper. Mix cornstarch with a little water, add to pan and cook for a further 10 minutes. Adjust seasoning to taste.

Transfer to a serving dish, garnish with celery leaves and serve with rice mixed with peas.

Preparation time 15 minutes plus marinating time

Cooking time 55 minutes

Serves 4

CARPACCIO OF BEEF

1 tablespoon olive oil
1¹/₄ lb (550 g) fillet of beef
1 small ripe avocado
4 tablespoons mayonnaise
juice of ¹/₂ lemon
1 cup (8 fl oz, 250 ml) beef stock
¹/₂ teaspoon Tabasco sauce
1 clove garlic
salt and freshly ground black
    pepper
chopped chives to garnish
mixed green leaf salad and potato
    salad to serve

Preheat oven to 425°F (220°C, Gas Mark 7). Heat oil in a small roasting pan. Turn beef in oil then cook in oven for 10 minutes; the beef should be very rare. Remove from oven, let stand until cold and chill to make beef easier to slice.

Put avocado, mayonnaise, lemon juice, stock, Tabasco, garlic, salt and pepper into a blender or food processor. Blend to a thin creamy sauce adding a little more stock if necessary.

Thinly slice the beef (a food slicer or electric carving knife is useful for this). Arrange beef decoratively on four large plates. Drizzle some avocado sauce over the beef and sprinkle with chopped chives. Serve the remaining sauce in a sauceboat. Serve with mixed green leaf salad and potato salad.

Preparation time 15 minutes plus chilling time

Cooking time 10 minutes

Serves 4

CHINESE BEEF AND VEGETABLE STIR-FRY

*1 oz (30 g) dried shiitake
    mushrooms, soaked in boiling
    water for 20 minutes*
2 tablespoons sunflower oil
*4 oz (115 g) snow peas
    (mangetout)*
4 oz (115 g) whole baby corn cobs
4 oz (115 g) bean sprouts
*1 large bunch scallions (shallots),
    chopped*
*1 red bell pepper (capsicum),
    seeded and sliced*
*1¼ lb (550 g) rib-eye steak,
    thinly sliced*
2 tablespoons oyster sauce
*2 tablespoons Chinese rice wine or
    dry sherry*
3 tablespoons light soy sauce
3 tablespoons beef stock
*1 tablespoon cornstarch
    (cornflour)*
fried rice or noodles to serve

Drain and dry mushrooms and cut in half if large.

Heat 1 tablespoon oil in a large frying pan or wok. Stir-fry mushrooms, snow peas, corn, bean sprouts, onions and bell pepper for 2–3 minutes, then remove from pan.

Heat remaining oil. Stir-fry beef for 2–3 minutes until brown. Return vegetables to pan. Mix together oyster sauce, rice wine, soy sauce, stock and cornstarch. Pour into pan, mix well, and bring to a boil stirring continuously.

Transfer to a warmed serving dish and serve immediately with fried rice or noodles.

Preparation time 20 minutes

Cooking time 10 minutes

Serves 4

COLD FOCACCIA SANDWICH

2 medium eggplants (aubergines),
   ends removed
3 tablespoons olive oil
1 large round focaccia bread,
   about 12 in (30 cm) in diameter
7 oz (200 g) smoked beef,
   pastrami or bresaola
1 oz (30 g) rocket (arugola)
1¹/₂ oz (45 g) piece fresh parmesan
   cheese
salt and freshly ground black
   pepper

Preheat broiler (grill) to high. Slice eggplant, brush both sides with oil, then broil (grill) for about 3 minutes each side until soft and brown. Let stand on paper towels until cold.

Slice focaccia in half horizontally, lay half the eggplant onto bottom half of bread, cover with beef and rocket. Shave parmesan over the top with a potato peeler and cover with remaining eggplant. Season lightly, cover with the top half of bread and cut into 8 slices.

Preparation time 10 minutes

Cooking time 10 minutes

Serves 4

FILLET STEAK TOSTADA

2 tablespoons olive oil
1 onion, finely chopped
1 clove garlic, crushed
1 tablespoon pickled sliced
    jalapeño peppers
grated rind and juice of 1 lime
2 large ripe tomatoes, peeled,
    seeded and chopped
7 oz (200 g) can corn kernels,
    drained
2 tablespoons chopped cilantro
    (fresh coriander leaves)
salt
4 fillet steaks, about 5–6 oz
    (150–175 g) each
1 tablespoon chili oil
4 tostadas
4 slices Monterey Jack, manchego
    or cheddar cheese

Heat oil in a frying pan and cook onion, garlic and peppers until onion is soft. Add lime rind and juice, tomatoes, corn, cilantro and salt. Mix well and keep salsa warm while cooking steaks.

Preheat broiler (grill) to high. Brush steaks each side with chili oil. Broil (grill) for 3–5 minutes each side; depending on how you like your steaks.

Place a steak in the middle of each tostada. Put a slice of cheese on top of each steak and return to broiler until cheese has melted. Put a tostada onto each of four plates and surround the steak with the salsa.

Preparation time 10 minutes

Cooking time 15 minutes

Serves 4

FIVE-SPICE BEEF SALAD

1 tablespoon sunflower oil
1 tablespoon sesame oil
1¹/₄ lb (550 g) rump steak, cut
    into strips
2 teaspoons grated fresh ginger
salt and freshly ground black
    pepper
2 teaspoons five-spice powder
1 teaspoon red chili pepper flakes
grated rind and juice of 1 orange
4 tablespoons guava or quince
    jelly
small bunch scallions (shallots),
    sliced
1 tablespoon cilantro (fresh
    coriander leaves), chopped
12 cup-shaped lettuce leaves
1 guava, peeled and thinly sliced

Heat oils together in a large frying pan or wok. Stir-fry beef for 2–3 minutes until brown and cooked through.

Add ginger, salt, pepper, five-spice powder, chili flakes, orange rind and juice and guava jelly to pan. Heat gently until jelly has melted and let stand until cold.

When mixture has cooled, stir in onions and cilantro.

Divide beef between lettuce cups. Put 3 lettuce cups onto each plate and garnish with guava slices.

Preparation time 15 minutes

Cooking time 5 minutes

Serves 4

GREEK-STYLE KEBABS

1/2 cup (4 fl oz, 120 ml) extra
virgin greek olive oil
juice of 1 lemon
1 tablespoon chopped fresh
oregano
1 tablespoon chopped fresh thyme
salt and freshly ground black
pepper
1 1/4 lb (550 g) rump steak, cut
into 16 cubes
12 oz (350 g) halloumi cheese, cut
into 12 cubes
12 cherry tomatoes

Mix together olive oil, lemon juice, oregano, thyme, salt and pepper in a ceramic or glass bowl.

Add cubed steak and cheese to marinade, mix well, cover and chill for at least 30 minutes or overnight.

Remove meat and cheese from marinade, reserving marinade.

Preheat broiler (grill) to high. Divide meat, cheese and tomatoes between 8 kebab skewers, beginning and ending with steak. Broil (grill) or barbecue for about 5 minutes, turning and brushing with marinade from time to time.

Preparation time 10 minutes plus marinating time

Cooking time 5 minutes

Serves 4

INSIDE-OUT BURGERS

1¹/₄ lb (550 g) lean ground
   (minced) beef
1 small onion, grated
salt and freshly ground black
   pepper
4 oz (115 g) soft blue cheese
   (dolcelatte or cambazola)
12 walnut halves
4 walnut bread rolls
red lettuce leaves to garnish
   (coral, radicchio or mignonette)

Mix beef, onion, salt and pepper and divide mixture into 8 flat burgers.

Slice cheese into four and put a slice onto 4 burgers.

Preheat broiler (grill) to high. Press 3 walnut halves into each slice of cheese and cover with remaining 4 burgers. Press the edges together very well to enclose the filling.

Broil (grill) or barbecue for about 5 minutes each side. Serve in walnut bread rolls, garnished with red lettuce leaves.

Preparation time 10 minutes

Cooking time 10 minutes

Serves 4

Japanese Stir-fried Beef

4 tablespoons akamiso (Japanese
    red soybean paste)
2 tablespoons Japanese soy sauce
2 tablespoons mirin (Japanese
    sweet sake)
1 tablespoon sesame oil
2 teaspoons soft brown sugar
1 tablespoon sunflower oil
1 teaspoon grated root ginger
1¹/₂ lb (700 g) thin end of beef
    fillet, cut into thin slices
4 teaspoons sesame seeds
udon noodles, umboshi plums,
    shredded daikon radish (mooli)
    to serve
scallion (green onion) tassels to
    garnish

Mix together akamiso, soy sauce, mirin, sesame oil and sugar to make a paste.

Heat sunflower oil in a large frying pan or wok, add ginger and beef, stir-fry for 2–3 minutes to seal meat.

Add akamiso paste, stir well and continue cooking until meat is coated with the sauce.

Divide meat between 4 warmed plates, sprinkle with sesame seeds. In each corner of the plate put a bundle of udon noodles, 2–3 umboshi plums, some shredded daikon radish and garnish with 3–4 onion tassels.

Preparation time 10 minutes

Cooking time 5 minutes

Serves 4

KESHI YENA

1 tablespoon sunflower oil
1 large onion, chopped
1 green bell pepper (capsicum),
    seeded and chopped
1½ lb (700 g) lean braising steak
    (chuck or blade), cut into small
    cubes
½–1 teaspoon dried red chili
    flakes or hot chili sauce
2 tomatoes, peeled and chopped
2 tablespoons tomato ketchup
    (sauce)
¼ cup (2 fl oz, 50 ml) water
salt and freshly ground pepper
2 oz (60 g) ready-to-eat prunes,
    chopped
2 oz (60 g) seedless raisins
2 tablespoons cucumber relish
1 tablespoon capers
10 oz (300 g) gouda cheese, sliced
    or 2 x 5 oz (150 g) packets
    gouda cheese slices
8 pimento-stuffed green olives,
    sliced

Heat oil in a large covered pan. Add onion, pepper and beef and cook for 2–3 minutes until beef is brown. Add chili, tomatoes, ketchup, water, salt and pepper. Bring to boil, lower heat, cover pan and simmer gently for 40 minutes, stirring occasionally.

Remove cover, and add prunes, raisins, relish and capers. Simmer uncovered for a further 10 minutes.

Preheat oven to 350°F (180°C, Gas Mark 4). Reserve 4 slices of cheese for top. Line 4 shallow individual ovenproof dishes with remaining cheese. Divide beef mixture between the dishes. Cut reserved cheese slices into lengthwise strips and arrange in a lattice pattern over beef. Put slices of olive between cheese lattice. Bake for 10 minutes. Serve immediately.

Preparation time 15 minutes

Cooking time 1 hour

Serves 4

KOFTAS WITH TAHINI DIP

1 small onion, chopped
2 tablespoons olive oil
2 oz (50 g) pine nuts
1¹/₂ lb (700 g) lean finely ground
  (minced) beef
1 teaspoon ground cinnamon
¹/₂ teaspoon ground allspice
1 teaspoon ground cumin
salt and freshly ground black
  pepper
1 tablespoon chopped flat leaf
  (Italian) parsley

Tahini dip:
4 tablespoons sesame paste
  (tahini)
1 clove garlic
²/₃ cup (5 fl oz, 150 ml) plain
  (natural) yogurt
juice of 1 large lemon
salt and freshly ground black
  pepper
2 tablespoons chopped fresh mint
pita (Lebanese) bread to serve

Cook onion in 1 tablespoon olive oil until soft. Add pine nuts and cook gently for 1–2 minutes until lightly browned. Transfer to paper towels to drain and cool.

Mix together beef, cinnamon, allspice, cumin, salt and pepper. Take 1 tablespoon beef, flatten it, put 1 teaspoon pine nut mixture and a pinch of parsley in middle. Form beef into a ball, making sure the join is well sealed. Continue to form balls with the remaining ingredients.

Preheat oven to 400°F (200°C, Gas Mark 6). Brush koftas with remaining oil. Cook on a rack over a baking pan for about 25 minutes. Drain on paper towels. Serve with tahini dip and pita breads.

For tahini dip: Put sesame paste, garlic, yogurt, lemon juice, salt and pepper into a blender or food processor and blend to a smooth sauce. Transfer to a small bowl and sprinkle with chopped mint.

Preparation time 20 minutes

Cooking time 30 minutes

Serves 4

KOREAN BEEF AND VEGETABLE STEAMBOAT

1 lb (450 g) daikon (mooli) radish,
    peeled and diced
salt
1 onion, chopped
1 clove garlic, chopped
1 tablespoon sesame oil
1 tablespoon sesame seeds
12 oz (350 g) lean ground
    (minced) beef
1 tablespoon soy sauce
$1/2$ teaspoon paprika
$1/4$ teaspoon cayenne pepper
1 egg, beaten
1 tablespoon sunflower oil
2 medium zucchini (courgette),
    ends removed and thinly sliced
bunch scallions (shallots), chopped
4 oz (115 g) mushrooms, sliced
8 oz (225 g) can bamboo, drained
12 oz (350 g) lean steak, cut into
    very thin strips
8 oz (225 g) bean curd, diced
4 cups (32 fl oz, 950 ml) Korean
    soup base or beef stock
1 red chili, seeded and chopped
Korean sticky rice and kim chee
    (Korean pickled cabbage) to
    serve

Cook daikon in lightly salted water for 10 minutes and drain. Heat sesame oil in a frying pan and cook onion and garlic for 2–3 minutes until onion is soft. Mix daikon with onion and sesame seeds.

Mix beef with soy sauce, paprika, cayenne and egg and form meat into 16–20 balls. Heat sunflower oil in a wok or frying pan and fry meat balls for about 10 minutes until brown and cooked through.

Mix together zucchini, onions, mushrooms and bamboo shoots.

In a Korean steamboat or a large fondue pan set over a burner, layer up half the daikon, half the steak, half the vegetables, half the bean curd and half the meat balls, then repeat the layering. Put soup base and chili into a pan, bring to a boil, and pour over meat and vegetables. Simmer at the table for about 5 minutes until steak is cooked and the vegetables are heated through. The steamboat can also be cooked on the stove in a heavy metal casserole dish that can be brought to the table. Serve with bowls of Korean sticky rice and kim chee.

Preparation time 20 minutes

Cooking time 25 minutes

Serves 4–6

LASAGNE WITH SPINACH AND RICOTTA

1 tablespoon sunflower oil
1 small onion, chopped
1 lb (450 g) lean ground (minced)
  beef
14 oz (400 g) can peeled tomatoes,
  chopped and juice reserved
1 teaspoon dried oregano
salt and freshly ground black
  pepper
1 teaspoon sugar
2 lb (900 g) fresh English spinach
  or 1 lb (450 g) frozen spinach
8 oz (225 g) ricotta cheese
1/2 teaspoon nutmeg
2 egg yolks
2 oz (60 g) freshly grated
  parmesan cheese
1 tablespoon cornstarch
  (cornflour)
1 1/4 cups (10 fl oz, 300 ml) low-fat
  (skim) milk
5 oz (150 g) instant green lasagne
  sheets

Heat oil in a large heavy-based frying pan and fry onion until soft. Add beef and cook until beef is no longer pink. Add tomatoes and juice from can, oregano, salt, pepper and sugar. Bring to a boil, reduce heat and cook uncovered for 20 minutes, stirring occasionally.

Cook spinach in 3 tablespoons of lightly salted water. Drain well and mix with ricotta, nutmeg, egg yolks and half the parmesan.

Mix cornstarch with a little of the milk. Add to remaining milk, bring to a boil and simmer for 2–3 minutes until slightly thickened. Season lightly.

Preheat oven to 350°F (180°C, Gas Mark 4). Lightly grease a shallow oblong baking dish. Layer half the lasagne, half the meat sauce and all the spinach mixture, then remaining meat sauce and lasagne. Spread the white sauce over the top.

Sprinkle with remaining cheese and bake in oven for 40 minutes.

Serve hot accompanied by fresh green salad, if liked.

Preparation time 20 minutes

Cooking time 1 hour

Serves 4

MEDITERRANEAN BEEF WITH GAZPACHO SALSA

2 cloves garlic
*1/2 cup (4 fl oz, 120 ml) passata
   (Italian sieved tomato sauce)*
3 tablespoons olive oil
*2 teaspoons herbes de Provence
   (mixture of thyme, rosemary,
   bay basil, savory)*
2 tablespoons red wine vinegar
salt and ground black pepper
1 3/4 lb (800 g) lean chuck steak

Gazpacho salsa:
1 small clove garlic
1 tablespoon red wine vinegar
2 tablespoons olive oil
1 tablespoon water
few drops Tabasco sauce
1 slice white bread, crusts removed
*4 ripe tomatoes, peeled, seeded
   and finely chopped*
*1 small green bell pepper
   (capsicum), seeded and finely
   chopped*
1/2 small cucumber, finely chopped
*1 small red (salad) onion, finely
   chopped*
*3 tablespoons roughly chopped
   flat-leaf (Italian) parsley*

Mix together garlic, passata, 2 tablespoons oil, herbes, vinegar, salt and pepper. Put beef into a shallow ceramic or glass dish. Cover with marinade, seal with a cover or plastic wrap and chill for 4 hours or overnight, turning the meat occasionally.

Preheat oven to 325°F (170°C, Gas Mark 3). Remove meat from marinade, reserving marinade. Pat meat dry with paper towels. In a heavy-based ovenproof dish that is also suitable for the stove top, heat remaining 1 tablespoon oil on stove and cook meat on both sides until browned. Add marinade, cover and cook in oven for about 1 hour. While meat is cooking make the salsa.

Gazpacho salsa: Put garlic, vinegar, oil, water, Tabasco, bread and half the tomatoes into a blender or food processor and blend to a smooth paste. Transfer to a bowl and add remaining tomatoes, bell pepper, cucumber, onion, parsley, salt and pepper. Mix well then cover and let stand for 30 minutes to allow tastes to amalgamate. Remove meat from oven. Cut into 4 pieces and arrange on a warmed serving plate. Strain marinade over the hot meat and serve with salsa.

Preparation time 20 minutes plus marinating time

Cooking time 1 hour

Serves 4

MEXICAN BEEF

1 large onion, chopped
1 clove garlic, crushed
2 red chili peppers, seeds removed
    and sliced
1 tablespoon sunflower oil
1 lb (450 g) ground (minced) beef
14 oz (400 g) can peeled tomatoes,
    chopped and juices reserved
2 teaspoons dried oregano
1 teaspoon cumin seeds
juice of $^1/_2$ lime
15 oz (425 g) can red kidney beans
$^3/_4$ cup (4 oz, 115 g) canned corn
    kernels
1 small, green bell pepper
    (capsicum), diced
2 tablespoons chopped cilantro
    (fresh coriander leaves)
salt and freshly ground black
    pepper
$3^1/_2$ oz (100g) packet tortilla or
    corn chips
3 oz (75 g) Monterey jack or
    cheddar cheese, grated
$^1/_2$ cup (4 fl oz, 120 ml) low-fat
    sour cream
sprigs cilantro (fresh coriander
    leaves) to garnish

Cook onion, garlic and chili peppers in oil until soft. Add beef and cook until meat is browned. Add tomatoes and juice from can, oregano, cumin and lime juice. Bring to a boil, reduce heat and simmer uncovered for 25 minutes, stirring occasionally.

Remove from heat and stir in kidney beans, corn, cilantro, salt and pepper.

Preheat oven to 400°F (200°C, Gas Mark 6). Transfer mixture to a shallow oblong ovenproof dish. Arrange tortilla chips in overlapping rows over the meat. Sprinkle with cheese and bake in oven for 15 minutes.

Drizzle with sour cream and serve garnished with fresh cilantro.

Preparation time 15 minutes

Cooking time 45 minutes

Serves 4

MINT AND HONEY BEEF WITH TWO SALSAS

2 tablespoons honey
2 tablespoons mint jelly
juice of 1 lemon
1 tablespoon sweet chili sauce
salt and ground black pepper
1³/₄ lb (800 g) thick piece rump
   steak, cut into 24 pieces
1 tablespoon sunflower oil
2 teaspoons cornstarch (cornflour)

Peach and papaya salsa:
1 small yellow bell pepper
   (capsicum), seeded and diced
1 peach, peeled, stoned and diced
1 small papaya (paw paw), peeled,
   seeded and finely diced
1 red chili pepper, seeded and cut
   into very thin strips
1 tablespoon lemon juice

Fennel, artichoke and olive salsa:
1 head Florence fennel about 6 oz
   (175 g), cored and finely
   chopped
4 oz (115 g) marinated artichoke
   hearts, chopped
1 tablespoon artichoke or olive oil
2 oz (60 g) pitted black olives,
   chopped
1 tablespoon chopped fresh mint

Mix together honey and mint jelly, lemon juice, chili sauce, salt and pepper in a large ceramic or glass bowl. Add meat, mix well, cover and chill for 4 hours or overnight.

Remove meat from marinade, reserving marinade. Heat oil in a large frying pan or wok, and stir-fry beef for about 4 minutes, stirring continuously as the meat will brown very quickly. Mix cornstarch with reserved marinade. Add to pan, mix well, and continue cooking for a further 2–3 minutes, stirring constantly until meat is coated with thick sauce. Transfer to 4 warmed plates and serve with the salsas.

Peach and papaya salsa: Combine all ingredients in a bowl, season to taste and transfer to a small serving dish.

Fennel, artichoke and olive salsa: Combine all ingredients in a bowl, then transfer to a small serving dish.

Preparation time 15 minutes plus marinating time

Cooking time 10 minutes

Serves 4

MUSTARD-BASTED BEEF

3 tablespoons French mustard
3 tablespoons soft brown sugar
2 tablespoons tarragon vinegar
1¹/2 lb (750 g) piece lean roasting
    beef (topside or top rump)
²/3 cup (4 oz, 115 g) small brown
    French (de Puy) lentils
1 onion, sliced
2 sticks celery, sliced
5 oz (150 g) oyster mushrooms
1 tablespoon (¹/2 oz, 15 g) butter
1 tablespoon chopped fresh
    tarragon
salt and freshly ground black
    pepper
1 tablespoon low-fat
    crème fraîche

Heat oven to 350°F (180°C, Gas Mark 4).

Mix together mustard, sugar and vinegar and spread over beef.
Put into a heavy-based ovenproof dish and cook in oven for
about 45 minutes, basting meat from time to time.

Meanwhile, in a saucepan, cook lentils in boiling water for
35–40 minutes until just tender. Drain well.

Melt butter in a frying pan and sauté onion and celery for
a few minutes until soft. Add mushrooms and cook for
2 minutes. Remove ovenproof dish from oven, take meat out
of dish and keep warm. Put ovenproof dish with cooking
juices onto the stove. Add lentils, onion mixture, tarragon,
salt, pepper and crème fraîche to pan juices, stir well and heat
gently until warmed through.

Transfer lentils to a serving dish. Thickly slice beef and arrange
over the top.

Preparation time 10 minutes

Cooking time 50 minutes

Serves 4

PICADILLO

1¹/₂ lb (700 g) lean ground
   (minced) beef
2 cups (16 fl oz, 500 ml) water
salt and freshly ground black
   pepper
1 onion, chopped
2 cloves garlic, crushed
1 green bell pepper (capsicum),
   seeded and chopped
2 green chili peppers, seeded and
   chopped
2 tablespoons sunflower oil
1 teaspoon ground cumin
2 tablespoons ketchup (tomato
   sauce)
1 tablespoon lemon juice
¹/₂ cup (4 fl oz, 120 ml) beef stock
2 oz (50 g) pimento-stuffed green
   olives, sliced
2 oz (50 g) seedless raisins
1 tablespoon chopped cilantro
   (fresh coriander leaves)
1 tablespoon chopped fresh
   parsley
1 tablespoon chopped oregano
rice and black beans to serve

Put meat into a large saucepan, cover with water and bring to a boil. Season with salt and pepper, cover pan, reduce heat and simmer for 20 minutes.

In a large frying pan, cook onion, garlic, bell pepper and chili in oil for 2–3 minutes until onion is soft.

When beef is cooked, drain well and add to frying pan along with cumin, ketchup, lemon juice, stock, olives and raisins. Mix well, bring to a boil, cover pan and cook for 10 minutes, stirring occasionally. Adjust seasonings to taste. Transfer to a warmed serving dish. Mix together fresh herbs and sprinkle over the top.

Serve with rice and black beans.

Preparation time 10 minutes

Cooking time 30 minutes

Serves 4

PIZZA BURGERS

1¼ lb (550 g) lean ground
    (minced) beef
2 oz (60 g) fresh white
    breadcrumbs
2 oz (60 g) pitted black olives,
    finely chopped
salt and freshly ground black
    pepper
1 red (salad) onion sliced
1 clove garlic, crushed
1 tablespoon olive oil
4 tablespoons sun-dried tomato
    paste
10 oz (275 g) jar artichoke hearts
    in oil, drained
1 teaspoon pizza herbs (mixed
    herbs)
4 oz (115 g) fontina cheese, sliced
Italian olive bread rolls
sprigs fresh basil to garnish

Preheat broiler (grill) to high. Mix together beef, breadcrumbs, olives, salt and pepper. Shape into 4 large flat burgers.

Broil (grill) burgers for 3–4 minutes each side.

Meanwhile, heat oil in a frying pan and sauté onion and garlic until onion is soft. Spread each burger with 1 tablespoon sun-dried tomato paste. Arrange artichokes and onion on top, sprinkle with herbs and place cheese on top.

Return to broiler and cook until cheese has melted and vegetables have heated through. Serve on Italian olive bread rolls garnished with fresh basil.

Preparation time 10 minutes

Cooking time 15 minutes

Serves 4

POLPETTES WITH VEGETABLE TAGLIATELLE

1¹/₄ lb (550 g) lean ground
    (minced) beef
1 small onion, grated
2 tablespoons grated fresh
    parmesan cheese
2 oz (60 g) fresh white
    breadcrumbs
2 tablespoons chopped fresh
    parsley
finely grated rind of 1 lemon
1 egg, beaten
salt and freshly ground black
    pepper
1 tablespoon olive oil
³/₄ cup (6 fl oz, 175 ml) beef stock
juice of ¹/₂ lemon
1 large bunch parsley
1 teaspoon cornstarch (cornflour)

Vegetable tagliatelle:
8 oz (225 g) long carrots, peeled
8 oz (225 g) celery root (celeriac),
    peeled
1 large leek, cut lengthwise into
    thin strips
¹/₂ oz (15 g) low-fat
    polyunsaturated margarine

Mix together beef, onion, cheese, breadcrumbs, chopped parsley, lemon rind, egg, salt and pepper. Form mixture into 12 large balls.

Heat oil in a large covered frying pan. Fry meat balls until evenly brown. Add stock and lemon juice, bring to a boil, reduce heat, cover pan and simmer gently for 20 minutes.

Remove meat balls from pan and keep warm. Put stock from pan into a blender or food processor with parsley and cornstarch and blend until smooth. Return to pan and bring to a boil, stirring continuously until thickened.

Divide meat balls between 4 warmed plates. Serve with parsley puree and vegetable tagliatelle.

For vegetable tagliatelle: Cut carrots and celery root into thin strips with a potato peeler, then cut again lengthwise into tagliatelle-sized strips. Mix with leek and blanch in lightly salted water for about 3 minutes. Drain well, toss in margarine and divide into 4 portions. Using 2 forks, twist each serving of vegetables into a knot to make 4 round bundles.

Preparation time 20 minutes

Cooking time 25 minutes

Serves 4

POT ROAST WITH LEEKS AND GREEN PEPPERCORNS

1 tablespoon sunflower oil

*1³/4 lb (800 g) silverside or bolar
    blade beef*

*1³/4 cups (10 fl oz, 300 ml) beef
    stock*

juice of ¹/2 lemon

*1 tablespoon green peppercorns in
    brine, drained*

salt

*1¹/2 lb (700 g) leeks, washed and
    sliced*

*1 tablespoon cornstarch
    (cornflour)*

*2 tablespoons low-fat crème
    fraîche*

Preheat oven to 325°F (170°C, Gas Mark 3). Heat oil in a heavy-based ovenproof dish on top of the stove and brown the beef. Add stock, lemon juice, peppercorns and salt. Bring to a boil, cover, put into oven and cook for 30 minutes. Add leeks and cook for a further hour. Remove from oven and keep meat warm while making the sauce.

Strain leeks and peppercorns, reserving stock. Spread half of them over a serving platter and keep warm. Put remaining leeks, peppercorns, stock, cornstarch (cornflour) and crème fraîche into a blender or food processor and blend until smooth. Transfer to a small saucepan, bring to a boil, stirring constantly. Reduce heat and simmer for 2–3 minutes until thickened.

Slice beef and arrange over leeks. Pour sauce down the middle of the beef.

Preparation time 15 minutes

Cooking time 1 hour 35 minutes

Serves 4

QUICK AND EASY STEAK SAUCES:

Pepper Steak, Steak with Cheat's Béarnaise Sauce and
Steak with Cranberry and Pine Nut Sauce

4 steaks (sirloin, rump or fillet),
    about 6–8 oz (175–225 g) each
1 tablespoon sunflower oil
salt and ground black pepper

Pepper sauce:
2 tablespoons crushed three-color
    peppercorns (green, pink and
    black)
2 tablespoons brandy
4 tablespoons low-fat crème
    fraîche

Cheat's béarnaise sauce:
1 tablespoon tarragon vinegar
2 tablespoons water
1 small shallot (spring onion),
    finely chopped
4 tablespoons low-fat mayonnaise
2 teaspoons finely chopped fresh
    tarragon

Cranberry and pine nut sauce:
2 tablespoons pine nuts
2 tablespoons cranberry sauce
2 tablespoons balsamic vinegar
3/4 cup (6 fl oz, 175 ml) beef stock
2 oz (60 g) dried cranberries

For pepper steak: Press peppercorns into both sides of the steaks. Pan-fry steaks in oil for 2–4 minutes each side until almost rare, medium or well-done, as liked. Pour brandy into pan, flame if desired. Add crème fraîche and salt and gently heat through.

Steak with cheat's béarnaise sauce: Heat broiler (grill) to high. Brush steaks with sunflower oil and broil (grill) for 2–4 minutes each side until rare, medium or well-done, as liked.

Meanwhile, put vinegar, water and onion into a small saucepan, bring to a boil then simmer until reduced to 1 tablespoon. Strain and discard onion. Put liquid back into pan with mayonnaise, tarragon, salt and pepper. Heat gently and serve with steaks.

Steak with cranberry and pine nut sauce: Pan-fry steaks in oil for 2–4 minutes each side until rare, medium or well-done, as liked. Remove from pan and keep warm.

Put pine nuts into pan and cook for 1 minute until lightly browned. Add cranberry sauce, vinegar, stock, dried cranberries, salt and pepper, bring to a boil then simmer for 2–3 minutes until sauce reduces slightly and becomes syrupy. Pour over steak.

Preparation time 5 minutes

Cooking time 10 minutes

Serves 4

QUICK BEEF AND PEPPER SOUP

2 tablespoons olive oil
1 onion, chopped
12 oz (350 g) lean braising steak
  (chuck or blade), cut into very
  small dice
1 tablespoon paprika
1 head Florence fennel, about 8 oz
  (225 g), cut into small dice
salt and freshly ground black
  pepper
4 cups (32 fl oz, 1 l) beef stock
1 large red bell pepper (capsicum),
  seeded and cut into diamond
  shapes
1 large yellow bell pepper
  (capsicum), seeded and cut into
  diamond shapes
2 tablespoons chopped fresh
  parsley to garnish

Heat oil in a large saucepan and sauté onion for about
2 minutes until soft. Add beef and cook until browned. Stir in
paprika, fennel, salt, pepper and stock and bring to a boil.
Cover pan, reduce heat and simmer for 20 minutes.

Add bell peppers and cook for a further 10 minutes. Divide
soup between 4 warmed soup bowls and sprinkle with
chopped parsley.

Preparation time 10 minutes

Cooking time 35 minutes

Serves 4

RED HOT BEEF

2 stalks lemon grass
1 large red chili pepper, seeded
 and chopped
1 teaspoon grated fresh ginger
2 cloves garlic
1 teaspoon ground coriander
1 teaspoon ground cumin
grated rind and juice of 1 lime
1 tablespoon paprika
1 teaspoon chili powder
1 cup (8 fl oz, 250 ml) coconut
 cream
2 tablespoons sunflower oil
1 1/2 lb (700 g) lean braising steak
 (chuck, blade or shin), diced
salt
2 onions, thinly sliced
2 red bell peppers (capsicums),
 seeded and thinly sliced
lime slices to garnish
sprigs cilantro (fresh coriander
 leaves) to garnish

Preheat oven to 325°F (170°C, Gas Mark 3).

Put lemon grass, chili pepper, ginger, garlic, coriander, cumin, lime rind and juice, paprika and chili powder into a blender or food processor with coconut cream. Blend until smooth.

Heat 1 tablespoon oil in a frying pan and fry beef until brown. Transfer to a heavy-based ovenproof dish, stir in spice mixture, season with salt, cover and cook in oven for 1 1/2 hours until very tender.

Cook onion and bell peppers in remaining oil in frying pan until soft. Stir into meat.

Transfer to warm serving dish and garnish with lime and cilantro.

Preparation time 15 minutes

Cooking time 1 1/2 hours

Serves 4

RED PESTO AND STEAK FOCACCIA

4 individual focaccia breads
4 tablespoons red pesto
4 minute steaks, about 4 oz
   (115 g) each
2 small avocados, peeled and
   seeded
12–16 basil leaves
7 oz (200 g) mozzarella cheese,
   sliced
salt and freshly ground black
   pepper

Cut breads in half horizontally and spread each half with
1/2 tablespoon red pesto.

Preheat broiler (grill) to high.

Broil (grill) steaks for 1–2 minutes each side. Place a steak onto bottom half of each bread. Cover each steak with half an avocado, sliced, 3–4 basil leaves and quarter of the mozzarella. Return to broiler and broil until cheese has melted and avocado is heated through. Season with salt and pepper. Cover with top half of bread, toasting under broiler if liked, and serve immediately.

Preparation time 10 minutes

Cooking time 5 minutes

Serves 4

ROAST BEEF STUFFED WITH FIGS AND GINGER

1 oz (30 g) low-fat
    polyunsaturated margarine
1 leek, thinly sliced
2 teaspoons grated fresh ginger
6 ready to eat dried figs, chopped
2 oz (60 g) fresh white
    breadcrumbs
1 tablespoon sesame seeds
salt and freshly ground black
    pepper
2 1/2 lb (1.25 kg) boned and rolled
    rib of beef
1 onion, sliced
6 black peppercorns
6 stalks parsley
3/4 cup (6 fl oz, 175 ml) green
    ginger wine
1 tablespoon all-purpose (plain)
    flour
3/4 cup (6 fl oz, 175 ml) beef stock
4–6 fresh figs to garnish

Heat margarine in a frying pan and cook leek and ginger for 2–3 minutes until leek is soft. Stir in figs, breadcrumbs, sesame seeds, salt and pepper. Mix well then let stand until cold.

Roll beef out flat and remove any excess fat if necessary. Spread fig stuffing over beef and roll up like a jelly-roll (Swiss roll). Tie securely with string.

Put onion, peppercorns and parsley into a large ceramic or glass bowl. Place meat on top and pour ginger wine over the top. Marinate, covered and chilled, for at least 4 hours or overnight, turning meat occasionally.

Preheat oven to 400°F (200°C, Gas Mark 6). Remove meat from marinade, reserving marinade. Pat meat dry with paper towels, place on a rack over a roasting pan and cook in oven for 1 1/2 hours.

Remove meat from oven and keep warm. Place roasting pan on stove. Stir flour into the pan juices. Add stock and reserved marinade. Bring to a boil, stirring constantly, then simmer for 2–3 minutes until slightly thickened.

Slice meat and arrange on a serving platter garnishing with fresh figs. Strain gravy into a sauceboat and serve with the meat.

Preparation time 20 minutes plus marinating time

Cooking time 1 3/4 hours

Serves 4–6

ROAST BEEF WITH A MUSTARD AND HERB CRUST

2¹/₂ lb (1.25 kg) piece lean beef rump
1 tablespoon olive oil
4 oz (115 g) fresh white breadcrumbs
4 tablespoons chopped fresh herbs, (parsley, thyme, oregano, basil, chervil etc)
1 clove garlic, crushed
2 tablespoons whole-grain mustard
salt and freshly ground black pepper
1 oz (25 g) low-fat polyunsaturated margarine, melted
1 egg white, lightly beaten
8 oz (225 g) carrots, cut into small dice
8 oz (225 g) kohl-rabi, cut into small dice
8 oz (225 g) leeks, sliced
8 oz (225 g) peeled and seeded acorn squash or similar squash, cut into small dice

Preheat oven to 375°F (190°C, Gas Mark 5). Heat oil in a frying pan and sear the meat, then transfer to a roasting pan and roast for 30 minutes.

Mix together breadcrumbs, herbs, garlic, mustard, salt and pepper. Stir in margarine and bind together with egg white.

Remove beef from oven, spread herb mixture over beef, then return to oven for a further 30–40 minutes, until crust is crisp and lightly browned.

Boil vegetables in lightly salted water for about 5 minutes until just cooked; strain.

Remove meat from oven, let stand for a few minutes, slice and arrange down the middle of a serving plate.

Spoon off any fat from the roasting pan, but retain meat juices. Add vegetables to roasting pan and toss in the juices.

Spoon half the vegetables down each side of the beef.

Preparation time 15 minutes

Cooking time 1¹/₂ hours

Serves 4–6

SAMOSAS WITH MINT AND YOGURT RAITA

1 small onion, finely chopped
1 clove garlic, crushed
1 tablespoon sunflower oil
8 oz (225 g) lean ground (minced) beef
1 teaspoon medium (Madras) curry powder
1 teaspoon ground cumin
1 teaspoon ground turmeric
1 teaspoon garam marsala
1 cup (8 fl oz, 225 ml) beef stock
1 medium potato, peeled and cut into small dice
salt and ground black pepper
2 oz (60 g) frozen petits pois (tiny peas)
8 large sheets phyllo pastry
3 oz (85 g) low-fat polyunsaturated margarine, melted
lime pickle to serve

Mint and yogurt raita:
1 cup (8 fl oz, 225 ml) low-fat plain (natural) yogurt
2 tablespoons finely chopped fresh mint
1 teaspoon garam marsala
mint sprigs

Heat oil in a large saucepan and sauté onion and garlic until soft. Add beef, curry powder, cumin, turmeric and garam marsala. Cook for 2–3 minutes until meat browns, then add stock, potato, salt and pepper. Cover pan and simmer gently for 20 minutes. Stir in petis pois and cook uncovered for 10 minutes until all liquid has evaporated. Let stand until cold.

Working with one sheet of phyllo at a time (keep the rest covered with a damp cloth), cut the sheet lengthwise into 4 strips. Brush one sheet with margarine and lay another sheet on top, brush this with margarine too. Put a tablespoon of beef in one corner of the pastry. Fold pastry and meat over to make a triangle, then continue folding at right angles to the end of the pastry. Make remaining triangles in the same way.

Preheat oven to 375°F (190°C, Gas Mark 5). Transfer triangles to a baking sheet, brush with margarine and cook in oven for 15 minutes until pastry is crisp and golden. Serve with mint and yogurt raita and lime pickle.

Mint and yogurt raita: Mix together yogurt, mint, salt and pepper. Transfer to a small bowl. Sprinkle with garam marsala and garnish with mint sprigs.

Preparation time 25 minutes

Cooking time 45–50 minutes

Serves 4

Satay Sticks with Cucumber and Sesame Salad

1 tablespoon sunflower oil
1 onion, finely chopped
1 clove garlic, crushed
1 red chili pepper, seeded and
    chopped or 1/2 teaspoon hot
    chili sauce
1/2 cup (4 fl oz, 120 ml) thick
    coconut cream
juice of 1/2 lemon
2 tablespoons soy sauce
4 tablespoons peanut butter
salt and freshly ground black
    pepper
11/2 lb (700 g) rump steak, cut
    into small cubes

Cucumber and sesame salad:
1 tablespoon sunflower oil
2 tablespoons sesame oil
juice of 1/2 lemon
salt and freshly ground black
    pepper
1 cucumber, peeled and cut into
    thick sticks
1 tablespoon sesame seeds, toasted

Heat oil in a saucepan and sauté onion, garlic and chili for about 2 minutes until onion is soft. Add coconut cream, lemon juice, soy sauce, peanut butter, salt and pepper. Bring to a boil, stirring constantly, then transfer to a ceramic or glass bowl and let stand until cold.

Add steak to the bowl, mixing well to coat thoroughly. Cover and chill for at least 30 minutes or overnight.

Divide meat cubes between 12 kebab skewers.

Preheat broiler (grill) to high. Broil (grill) or barbecue for about 5 minutes, turning frequently.

Serve with cucumber and sesame salad.

For cucumber and sesame salad: In a serving bowl, mix oils, lemon juice, salt and pepper. Add cucumber, mix well and sprinkle with sesame seeds.

Preparation time 20 minutes plus marinating time

Cooking time 10 minutes

Serves 4

SINGAPORE NOODLES

9 oz (250 g) rice stick noodles
7 oz (200 g) broccoli, cut into
    small florets
4 oz (115 g) thin asparagus spears
salt
2 tablespoons sunflower oil
1 lb (450 g) top rump steak, cut
    into long thin strips
4 oz (115 g) bean sprouts
1 lb (450 g) pak choi (Chinese
    broccoli), thick stems removed
2 tablespoons sesame oil
3 tablespoons soy sauce
3 tablespoons sweet chili sauce

Put noodles into a large saucepan and cover with boiling water. Bring back to boil, remove from heat and let stand for 8–10 minutes until tender.

Blanch broccoli and asparagus in lightly salted boiling water for 2 minutes; drain well.

Heat sunflower oil in a large frying pan or wok. Stir-fry the beef for 2–3 minutes until brown. Add broccoli, asparagus, bean sprouts and pak choi and stir-fry for a further 2-3 minutes until heated through.

Strain noodles, rinse with boiling water and drain well. Add to the frying pan. Mix well, then stir in sesame oil, soy and chili sauces.

Transfer to a warm serving dish and serve immediately.

Preparation time 15 minutes

Cooking time 10 minutes

Serves 4

STEAMED STEAKS WITH CARROT AND ZUCCHINI RIBBONS

1 tablespoon sunflower oil
4 porterhouse steaks, about 6 oz
    (175 g) each
2 medium carrots, peeled
2 medium zucchini (courgettes),
    ends removed
4 teaspoons whole-grain mustard
salt and freshly ground black
    pepper
sprigs fresh chervil to garnish
Sauce:
2 shallots (spring onions), finely
    chopped
4 teaspoons whole-grain mustard
salt and freshly ground black
    pepper
1 cup (8 fl oz, 250 ml) beef stock
1/2 cup (4 fl oz, 125 ml) light
    (single) cream

Heat oil in a frying pan and fry steaks for 1-3 minutes each side, depending how you like them. Remove steaks from pan and drain on paper towels, reserving oil in pan.

With a potato peeler, cut along the length of each carrot and zucchini to make thin ribbons. Lay out 4 sheets of plastic wrap and make a square of alternate ribbons of carrot and zucchini, slightly overlapping, lengthwise on each piece of plastic wrap. Spread each with whole-grain mustard and season with salt and pepper.

Place a steak into the middle of each vegetable square. Use the plastic wrap to fold the vegetables over steaks. Wrap each steak tightly in plastic wrap and fold the edges under. Put the parcels into a steamer set over a pan of boiling water and steam for 5 minutes.

To make the sauce, soften onions in reserved oil in the frying pan. Add mustard, salt, pepper and stock, bring to a boil, then simmer for 2-3 minutes to reduce slightly. Stir in cream. Heat gently. Divide sauce between four warmed plates. Carefully unwrap steaks, put one into the middle of each plate and garnish with chervil.

Preparation time 10 minutes

Cooking time 10-12 minutes

Serves 4

STUFFED VINE LEAVES

12 oz (350 g) lean ground
   (minced) beef
1 onion, finely chopped
1 clove garlic, crushed
3 oz (75 g) lean bacon, diced
1 tablespoon olive oil
1¼ cups (10 fl oz, 300 ml) beef
   stock
salt and freshly ground black
   pepper
6 oz (175 g) vine leaves
4 oz (115 g) cooked rice
1 tablespoon chopped parsley
1 teaspoon chopped oregano
4 oz (115 g) canned chestnuts,
   chopped
1 tablespoon tomato ketchup
   (sauce)
1 tablespoon lemon juice
2 teaspoons cornstarch (cornflour)
lemon slices to garnish
sprigs oregano to garnish

Heat oil in a large saucepan and fry beef, onion, garlic and bacon for 2-3 minutes until beef browns. Add stock, salt and pepper, and bring to a boil. Reduce heat, cover and simmer for 20 minutes.

Put vine leaves into a saucepan of boiling water, simmer gently for 5 minutes. Strain, cool under running water and drain well.

Strain the meat, reserving stock. Mix meat with rice, parsley, oregano and chestnuts.

Preheat oven to 375°F (180°C, Gas Mark 5). Place vine leaves vein side up with the stem towards you. Put a tablespoon of beef into the middle of each leaf, fold the stem edge up, fold in sides and roll up to make a cigar shape. Continue with remaining vine leaves and rice.

Pack vine leaves tightly in a shallow ovenproof dish making sure the joins are underneath.

In a small pan, mix together reserved stock, ketchup, lemon juice and cornstarch, bring to a boil then pour over vine leaves. Cover dish and cook in oven for 30 minutes.

Serve garnished with lemon slices and oregano.

Preparation time 20 minutes

Cooking time 50 minutes

Serves 4

SUKIYAKI

1¹/₄ lb (550 g) fillet steak, cut into
     paper thin slices
4 oz (115 g) shiitake mushrooms
6 oz (175 g) young leeks, thinly
     sliced diagonally
6 oz (175 g) Chinese (celery)
     cabbage, shredded
7 oz (200 g) bean sprouts
8 oz (225 g) tofu, diced
7 oz (200 g) cooked shirataki
     noodles
1 cup (8 fl oz, 250 ml) water
4 tablespoons sunflower oil
individual bowls of cooked
     Japanese rice to serve

Sauce:
2 tablespoons mirin (Japanese
     sweet sake)
2 tablespoons sake
2 tablespoons soy sauce
1 tablespoon instant dashi powder
1 teaspoon brown sugar

Sukiyaki is traditionally cooked at the table either in an electric frying pan or a heavy frying pan set over a burner with each guest cooking their individual portion.

Arrange beef, vegetables, tofu and noodles attractively on serving dishes, with a bowl of Japanese rice for each individual.

Sauce: Mix together mirin, sake, soy sauce, dashi powder, sugar and water in a small pan, and bring to a boil. Transfer to a small jug and bring to the table.

Heat 1 tablespoon oil in the frying pan, and add a quarter of the beef. Cook quickly then remove to rice bowls. Add a quarter of the vegetables, a quarter of the tofu and a quarter of the noodles to pan, stir fry quickly, moistening with a little sauce throughout. Repeat with the remaining ingredients. If it is not possible to cook sukiyaki at the table, cook all ingredients together in a wok on the stove, transfer to a warmed serving dish and serve immediately.

Preparation time 10 minutes

Cooking time 10 minutes

Serves 4

THAI BEEF SALAD

1 tablespoon chopped fresh mint
2 tablespoons chopped cilantro
    (fresh coriander leaves)
1 tablespoon chopped fresh basil
1 tablespoon grated galangal or
    fresh root ginger
2 tablespoons Thai sweet chili
    sauce
1 tablespoon Thai fish sauce
1 tablespoon lime juice
1 thin stalk lemon grass
4 fresh Kaffir lime leaves, middle
    stalk removed
salt and ground black pepper
3 tablespoons sunflower oil
1¼ lb (550 g) sirloin or fillet
    steak, thinly sliced
4 oz (115 g) bean sprouts
4 oz (115 g) button mushrooms
    (champignons), thinly sliced
1 bunch scallions (shallots), cut
    lengthwise into thin strips
1 large carrot, cut lengthwise into
    thin strips
4 oz (115 g) canned water
    chestnuts, thinly sliced
2 oz (60 g) dry roast peanuts,
    roughly chopped

Put mint, cilantro, basil, galangal, chili sauce, fish sauce, lime juice, lemon grass, lime leaves, salt, pepper and 2 tablespoons oil into a blender or food processor, blend until smooth and transfer to a large ceramic or glass bowl.

Heat remaining oil in a large frying pan or wok. Quickly stir-fry beef for 2-3 minutes until brown. Add to bowl, mix well and let stand until cold.

Mix together beansprouts, mushrooms, onions, carrot and water chestnuts.

Make a nest of vegetables on a large round serving platter. Put beef salad in the middle and sprinkle with peanuts.

Preparation time 15 minutes plus cooling time

Cooking time 2-3 minutes

Serves 4

BEAUTIFUL BEEF — EACH TIME

DRY HEAT COOKING METHODS

PAN-FRYING

Pan-frying is a very quick and healthy method of cooking beef. If using a non-stick pan it is usually unnecessary to add any extra oil. Pan-frying is most suitable for steaks such as rump, sirloin or rib-eye. Depending on the thickness of the meat it takes 2–3 minutes each side for rare meat and up to 5–6 minutes each side for well done meat. An accompanying sauce can be made in the pan utilizing the meat juices (see Quick and Easy Steak Sauces, recipe page 84).

STIR-FRYING

Stir-frying is probably the quickest method of cooking beef. Use the most tender cuts, such as filet or rump, cut into thin slices or strips. Always stir-fry in a hot, lightly-oiled wok or large frying pan that allows room for the meat to be tossed around. Cook the meat in small batches if necessary. It should take 2–3 minutes (see Chinese Beef and Vegetable Stir-fry, recipe page 46).

BROILING (GRILLING)

Broiling is a direct heat method, suitable for steaks and kebabs. Always preheat the broiler, brush the meat with oil if necessary, then put onto a broiling pan. The meat should be sealed by placing near the heating element but lowering the pan or reducing the heat as necessary to finish cooking, depending on the thickness of the meat or how you like it cooked. Cooking times are similar to pan-frying (see Fillet Steak Tostada, recipe page 50).

BARBECUING

Barbecuing is probably the most sociable way of cooking beef. Barbecues need time to preheat, but meat cooking times are the same as conventional broiling. Steaks or kebabs should be marinaded if possible, but all meat will have the added taste of charcoal or woodsmoke (see Satay Sticks with Cucumber and Sesame Salad, recipe page 98).

OVEN ROASTING

Oven roasting is a very easy method of cooking beef. Although taking more time to cook, very little preparation is necessary. Beef is best roasted on a rack over a roasting pan, allowing any excess fat in the meat to drain off. The most suitable cuts are ribs, topside, or bolar blade. Check with the individual recipes for oven temperatures and cooking times (see Roast Beef Stuffed with Figs and Ginger, recipe page 92).

MOIST HEAT COOKING METHODS

POT-ROASTING

Pot-roasting is suitable for the tougher joints of beef, such as brisket or silverside, that require long, slow, moist cooking to make them tender. The meat should be sealed in oil then liquid added to half cover the meat, which should be turned occasionally. Vegetables can be cooked in the pan to produce a complete meal. Pot roasts can be cooked in a slow oven or simmered on top of the stove (see Pot Roast with Leeks and Green Peppercorns, recipe page 82).

CASSEROLING

This is a very good method for cooking beef dishes where tastes need to be absorbed, such as curries. Chuck, blade, and skirt are all suitable cuts to use and can be diced or sliced. Do not add too much liquid to a casserole as meat and vegetables give out quite a lot of liquid during cooking. Casseroles can be cooked in the oven or on top of the stove (see Caribbean Beef Stew, recipe page 42).

INDEX